ACTION HISTORY

The Invaders

S T E V E   B U X T O N

Acknowledgements

The publishers would like to thank the following for their permission to reproduce copyright illustrations:

Ancient Art and Architecture Collection p6, 7, 10, 15, 19 bottom, 28 right, 34, 38 right, 40 all, 48;
Supplied by Balfour Beatty p11 right;
Bath Archaeological Trust p12 top right;
Reproduced by Courtesy of the Trustees of the British Museum p5 both;
Cambridge University Collection: copyright reserved, p18;
Colchester and Essex Museum p14;
Sonia Halliday Photographs p11 left, 21 right;
Michael Holford Photographs p30 both;
A F Kersting p43;
The Mansell Collection p12;
The Master and Fellows of University College, Oxford p38 bottom left;
National Trust/Walton p8;
The Society of Antiquaries of London p19 top.

British Library Cataloguing in Publication Data
Buxton, Steve
  The Invaders.
  1. Great Brtain to 1066.
  I. Title
  941.01

  ISBN 0–340–51898–7

First published 1991
Impression number 10 9 8 7 6 5 4 3 2
Year   1998 1997 1996 1995 1994 1993

©1991 Steve Buxton
Illustration by Joseph McEwan

Typeset by Taurus Graphics, Kidlington, Oxon.
Printed in Hong Kong for the educational publishing division of Hodder & Stoughton Ltd, Mill Road, Dunton Green, Sevenoaks, Kent TN13 2YA by Colorcraft Ltd.

Contents

1 The Roman Empire

primitive, advanced, conquered, south,
west, east, north, empire, weapon

Two thousand years ago Britain was a very
primitive land covered in forests. There were
very few people here. They lived in huts.

But in the lands around the Mediterranean sea
there were more advanced peoples. You can see
some of their cities marked on the map. Some of
the place names are still used. Some disappeared
long ago.

The Roman Empire

The Romans

One of the cities was becoming more powerful
and wealthy than the others. The people of Rome
had a strong army. They started wars and
conquered other cities and lands to the south of
Rome. See if you can find Sicily and Carthage on
the map. These were the first places Rome
conquered.

Then the Romans conquered lands to the west
and east – places like Greece and Macedonia.
Lastly the Roman armies moved north to conquer
parts of Britain.

It took a long time to conquer all of these
places. Over 200 years. All the lands which were
ruled by the Romans became part of the Roman
Empire.

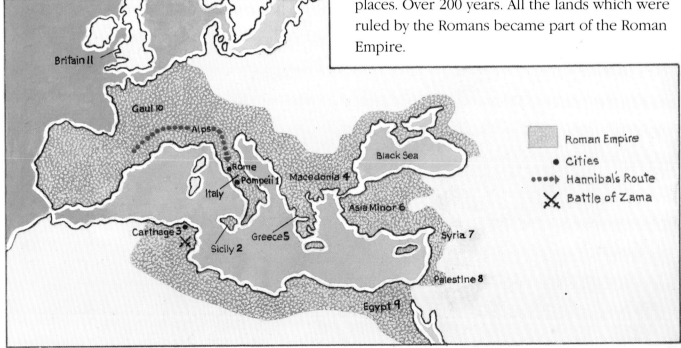

Britain 11
Gaul 10
Alps
Rome
Pompeii 1
Italy
Sicily 2
Carthage 3
Greece 5
Macedonia 4
Black Sea
Asia Minor 6
Syria 7
Palestine 8
Egypt 9

Roman Empire
• Cities
●●●●▶ Hannibal's Route
✕ Battle of Zama

Rome Fights Carthage

The Romans found it very hard to conquer Carthage. Like Rome, Carthage was a very rich city with a good army. The Romans got a shock when they tried to threaten Carthage.

Hannibal

Hannibal was a fine general. He was in charge of Carthage's army. He did not wait for the Romans to attack. Instead he led his army to Italy to attack Rome. He took a difficult route through the Alps mountains. He was able to surprise the Romans by attacking them from the north (see map).

Using his secret weapon he beat the Roman armies time after time. He led his army to the walls of Rome itself but he did not have enough soldiers to capture the city.

On the right is a coin from Carthage showing Hannibal and his 'secret weapon'

Rome Fights Back

Slowly the Roman army fought back but it took three years for them to force Hannibal out of Italy. Hannibal was pushed back to Carthage. Five years later his army was finally beaten by the Romans in a battle at Zama near to Carthage (see map). Carthage became part of the Roman Empire. Hannibal killed himself so that he would not be taken prisoner.

WORKFILE

1 Look at the map.

a Write down two place names which are still used today.

b Write down two place names which you do not think are still used

c What do we now call the Roman country Gaul?

2 Look again at the map. Each place name has a number. The numbers show the order in which the Romans conquered other places.

In the correct order make a list of all the places which became part of the Roman Empire. Give your list the title 'Places Conquered By The Romans'.

3 Copy and complete these sentences. Choose the correct words from those in brackets.

a Two thousand years ago Rome was one of many cities in the lands around the _____ sea. (Mediterranean, Atlantic, Black)

b Rome became stronger because it had a fine _____ . (navy, army, airforce)

c Romans took over _____ years to build their empire. (5, 20, 200)

d At this time Britain was a very _____ country. (advanced, primitive, powerful)

e Britain was one of the _____ places the Romans tried to conquer. (biggest, last, nearest)

4 Look at the pictures of the coin. Draw a picture of Hannibal's secret weapon.

2 *Roman Buildings*

memorial, designer, columns, arches, ruin, archaeologist, remains, patience, dig, site

Roman builders were very skilled. The city of Rome was full of beautiful stone buildings. So were other places in the Empire. There were palaces and temples, public buildings and memorials to famous Romans.

Roman designers used many columns, arches and carvings.

A few Roman buildings still remain. This archway still stands in Rome. It was built as a memorial to a Roman leader. But most Roman buildings have long since fallen down and disappeared. Their ruins are waiting to be discovered by archaeologists.

Roman archway,
Rome

Archaeologists

Hello, I'm an archaeologist, a special sort of historian. I study old remains, bits of the past that are buried underground.

It takes a lot of skill and patience to 'dig' a site. We find all sorts of things. Bits of old buildings, jewellery, pottery and bones.

Then we have to try to work out what life was like in the area long ago.

I think I've found something.

trowel • sieve • brush

Archaeologists at work

WORKFILE

1 Look carefully at the picture of the Roman arch. Answer these questions in sentences.

a How tall do you think the building is? Use the people in the picture to help you guess its height in metres.

b How many columns can you see?

c How many arches can you see?

d What material do you think the arch is built out of?

2 Look at the tools used by the archaeologist.

Write a sentence about each one to say what you think they are used for. Try to use some of these words.

Trowel – dig, soil, cover, remains.
Brush – clean, remains, found.
Sieve – sift, soil, missed.

3 Some remains last a long time in the ground. Some rot away before they are found. Copy this table. Put a tick by each object to say whether you think it will last a long time or a short time in the earth.

Object	long time	short time
coins		
stone vases		
pottery		
leather sandals		
gold jewellery		
wooden spoon		
cloth tunic		
wooden cartwheel		

3

Home Comforts

hypocaust, villa, mosaic, pillars

In cold countries the Romans invented 'Hypocaust', under-floor heating to keep them warm. This type of floor still exists at the site of a Roman villa in England.

The hypocaust at Chedworth Villa

How it Worked

One or two of my slaves keep the fire going. The smoke and hot air go under the floor and warm the room above. So in freezing Britain I keep nearly as warm as I did in Rome.

If you Romans like it hot you should come down here!

WORKFILE

1 Look carefully at the photograph of the hypocaust and complete the following table. Try to find each item in the photograph. Write its number in the table.

2 Draw your own diagram to show how a hypocaust works. Put labels on your diagram.

3 Copy this cartoon of a Roman in England. Fill in the speech bubble to show why he might want hypocaust heating.

Item	Picture number
Doorway	
Stone walls	
Mosaic floor	
Missing floor	
Hypocaust pillars to hold up floor	
Space under floor for hot air to pass through	

4

Roads and Towns

ruined, exists, plan

Look carefully at the picture below. It shows a ruined Roman street which still exists at Pompeii in Italy.

A Pompeii street

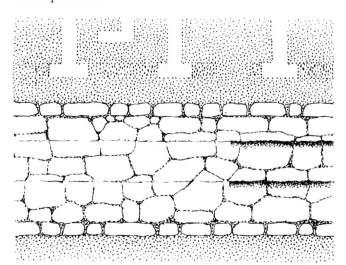

Plan of a Pompeii street

WORKFILE

1 Write an archaeologist's report to show what you can see. Copy this report choosing the correct details to complete the sentences.

Site report. Pompeii, Italy
Date _____
Archaeologist _____ . (name)

Roman roads in this town were (badly/ carefully) built out of (concrete/flat stones/ tarmac).

There are ruins of (shops/baths/farms) near the road. These were (badly/strongly) built out of (wood/bricks/stone).

People could (travel along/cross) the road on (two/three/four) raised stepping stones. Marks in the road show that it was often used by (horses/carts/people).

The road (has good drains/might get flooded in wet weather).

---

2 Draw a plan to go with your report. Put labels on your plan. Use the plan opposite to help you.

Careful, there is something missing from the plan. Look at the picture again. Use these labels:

Pavement,   Walls of ruined buildings,
Ruts in road made by cart wheels,
Stepping stones for crossing road in wet weather,
Flat stones carefully fitted together.

Water

aqueduct, engineer

The aqueduct at Nimes in France

To keep people healthy the Romans supplied their towns with clean water. Aqueducts were built to carry the water from the countryside.

This acqueduct still stands in France. The water ran along a channel. This was like a large gutter dug into the top of the aqueduct. See how the Roman designers and engineers have used arch shapes to carry the weight. They had worked out that these were very strong. But they were hard to build.

WORKFILE

1 Draw a picture of a Roman aqueduct. Make up a title.

2 Look at this picture of a modern bridge being built and compare it with the Roman aqueduct. Can you find the concrete pillars holding up the bridge? What other building materials is being used? Clue – read the caption under the picture.

Repairs on a viaduct on the M62 – using steel to strengthen the bridge

3 Copy the table below. Tick the correct column to show what materials were used by the Roman and modern day engineers. Some materials may have two ticks.

Material	Roman	Modern
steel		
concrete		
bricks		
stone		
wood		
cement		

5 Roman Women

evidence

Archaeologists have found many pieces of evidence from Roman Britain. Let us use some of these to try to learn a little about the life of a rich Roman woman.

Look carefully at this evidence. Source A is a Roman picture carved in stone. Source B is a photo of a Roman brooch found by archaeologists.

Source A

A Roman carving

Source B

A woman's brooch

WORKFILE

1 Study Source A. Then copy and complete these sentences. Choose the correct endings from those in brackets.

a The woman is visiting a _____ (hairdressers, dentist, clothes shop).

b Her chair is made of _____ (leather, basketwork, wood).

c The girl is holding a _____ (mirror, hat, hairdryer).

2 Look at the list below. It shows many of the different ways we fasten our clothes. Copy down those which you think have been invented SINCE Roman times. Use the sources to help you. (Do the others in your group agree with you?)

Zips, pins, laces, press studs, belts, buttons, velcro, hooks, buckles, safety pins.

Source C

Source C shows what a Roman woman's dressing table might have looked like. It is a modern photograph but most of the items are Roman and have been found by archaeologists.

3 Study Source C carefully.

a Look at the numbered items. Then copy and complete this table.

In the first empty column write what you think the item is. In the second empty column write what you think it was used for. Choose from:

Bottles, mirror, necklace, bracelet, ring, hairpin, brooch, lamp, nail cleaners, spoon, pin cushion, tweezers.

b Choose one item from the list which you think was not found by archaeologists. Write a sentence to explain your choice. (Do the others in your group agree with you?)

Item number	Name	Used for
1		
2		
3		
4		
5		
6		
7		
8		
9		
10		
11		
12		

c Make a list of 20 items which you or your family own (for example clothes, shoes). Think about these items. Are there any parts which might last for two thousand years? Tick the ones you think might/could be found by future archaeologists.

6 *The Roman Legions*

legion, tribe, barbarian, chariot, infantry

Marcus Facilis was a real person. His tombstone was found in England.

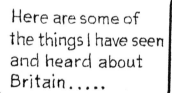

I am Marcus, proud officer in the Roman army. I hear my legion will soon leave Rome. We are going to conquer the tribes who live in the far off island of Britain. I have heard a lot about Britain. There will be much glory if we conquer the lands, but I'm not sure that I want to go.

Here are some of the things I have seen and heard about Britain.....

Source A:

1   'Britain is distant and wild. The climate is
2   awful with frequent rain and mists.
3   The British are barbarians but they show
4   spirit. Some fight from chariots but their
5   strength is their infantry.
6   It is seldom that two or three tribes
7   combine to drive off danger. Fighting in
8   separate groups they are all conquered.

Written by Tacitus, a Roman Historian

Source B: 'The British make fine jewellery.'

Source C: 'I don't think much of their towns.'

Source D: 'The Britons are good fighters and use chariots.'

WORKFILE

1 Make a (labelled) drawing of a Roman soldier.

2 Read Source A carefully. Copy this table and find the lines from Source A which prove that the statements in column one are true. Write down the numbers of the correct lines in column two.

Column one: statement	Column two: line number
The Romans did not like the British weather.	
The British have put up a good fight.	
The British tribes did not get together to fight their enemies.	
The British had good foot soldiers.	

3 Look at Source C. Compare this settlement with what you know about Roman cities and buildings, for example, Pompeii. See how many differences you can find.

Think about: Size of buildings
Design and shape of buildings
Building materials
Building skills

(Do the others in your group agree with you?)
Write two or three sentences to sum up the differences you have spotted.

Source E: 'There are many different tribes in Britain. I hope they don't all get together to fight us.'

Selgovae
Novantae
Brigantes
Ordovices
Coritani
Icenni
Silures
Dobunni
Trinovantes
Catuvellauni
Cantii
Durotriges
Regnenses
Dumnonii

WORKFILE

1 Look at Source E. How many tribal kingdoms were there in Britain? Make a list of their names.

2 Copy one of the pictures of a Briton shown below. Add on some of the jewellery which he/she might have worn. Use Source F to help you.

Source F:
The men as well as the women wear bracelets on their wrists and arms and thick rings of gold around their necks. They wear finger rings and even golden tunics. They have striped cloaks fastened with buckles.'

Written by Siculus, a Greek traveller.

Look again at sources A to F. They show you some of the ideas Marcus has in his mind when he thinks about Britain.

Copy the picture below and write in Marcus's thoughts and ideas. Two have been done for you.

On the left-hand side write those thoughts which would make him happy to go to Britain.

On the right-hand side write those thoughts which might put him off.

The Roman army is the finest in the world by far

I do not think I will like the weather

Choose from these ideas. Out of each pair only one idea is true.

'The Roman army is the finest in the world by far'
or
'The British tribes have better armies than us'

'There will be plenty of gold and silver to capture'
or
'There will not be much treasure to bring back'

'It should be easy to conquer all the separate tribes'
or
'It will be very difficult because all the tribes fight together'

'There will be fine cities to capture'
or
'We will have to build our own houses and baths'

'I will like the weather'
or
'I do not think I will like the climate'

7 *The Roman Army in Britain*

> **invaded, rebelled, Latin, toga**

The Romans invaded Britain three times. The first two times they won battles but left soon afterwards. The third invasion took place in the year 43 AD.

Forty thousand Roman soldiers crossed the English Channel. One by one the British tribes were beaten in many battles. There was some hard fighting. The British moved back into their 'hill forts' which were difficult to capture.

Source A

Maiden Castle hill fort

WORKFILE

1 Look at Source A. These are the remains of a British hill fort. Find the ramparts (banks of earth).

The Britons used these to protect the middle area (4). The Romans had to attack up hill to capture each rampart one by one. Write a sentence or two to say:

a How many entrances can you find through the ramparts?

b How high do you think the ramparts are? Use other clues in the picture to help you guess, such as trees.

c If you were the Roman commander, which side of the fort would you attack – 1, 2 or 3? Why?

Look at Source B. Archaeologists have found this evidence of the fighting between Romans and Britons. This seems to be part of a Roman weapon dug into a Briton's back bone.

Source B

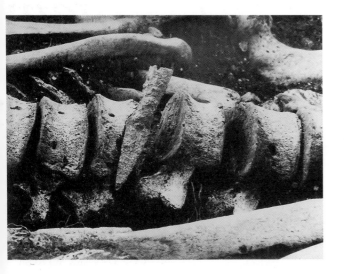

Slowly the Romans conquered southern Britain. They also won battles against tribes in the north and west of Britain. But before the Roman army could reach the far north, it had to return back to south. The Romans did not have enough soldiers to cover all of the country.

The conquered tribes sometimes rebelled against their new Roman rulers. Queen Boudicca led a famous rebellion by the Icenni tribe. For a while the Romans were worried. The Icenni captured several Roman towns and burnt them down. But in the end the Roman army beat them in a bloody battle. Eighty thousand Icenni were killed but only four hundred Roman troops died.

After the tribes were beaten the Romans tried to keep the peace. One Roman leader in Britain was called Agricola.

Source C

'Agricola tried to get the British used to a life of peace and quiet. He built temples, public squares and good houses.

He educated the sons of British chiefs. Instead of hating Latin they became eager to speak it.

The toga was seen everywhere. The people learned to like baths and feasts and gave up war.'

Roman Baths
at Bath

WORKFILE

1 Copy this paragraph and fill in the missing words:

Choose from these words.

army, south, tribes, Boudicca, 43, lifestyle, Britons.

The main Roman invasion took place in the year _____ AD. A large Roman _____ took part which was very powerful. One by one the _____ in the _____ of Britain were conquered though the Romans never controlled all of Britain. Queen _____ led a rebellion against the Romans but her army was defeated in a few months. Soon many _____ forgot about fighting the Romans. They enjoyed the better _____ which Roman rule had brought for many of them.

2 Copy these questions and their answers. Choose the correct answer from those given. Put a ring around it.

  a Which part of Britain was captured first by the Romans? (north, south, east, west)

  b Which part never came under Roman control? (far north, far south, midlands)

3 Read Source C carefully. How did the Romans try to make Britain peaceful?

  Copy this table. Decide which methods the Romans used. Put a tick by them in the 'yes' column. Tick 'no' for those the Romans did not try.

(Do the others in your group agree with you?)

Methods tried by the Romans	yes	no
Built fine public buildings for the people.		
Paid the British a lot of money.		
Gave the British some new chariots.		
Taught the British to speak Latin.		
Built good houses and towns.		
Left the British to rule themselves.		
Trained the British to fight better.		
Taught the British to wear Roman clothes.		

8 Keeping Control of Britain

centurion, frostbite, promotion

After the Romans had conquered parts of Britain they built forts for their soldiers to live in. They built roads for their armies to march along. They could reach any trouble spots quickly. The ruins of many forts and roads can still be seen today.

Source A
Roman towns and roads

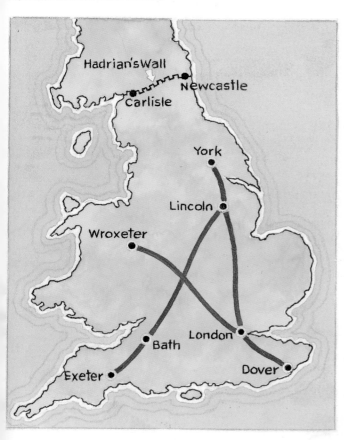

Hadrian's Wall

Some of the best evidence of the Romans in Britain is found in the north of England. The Roman emperor Hadrian ordered a wall to be built. It was about five metres high and stretched across the country from coast to coast. It was guarded by soldiers. They tried to keep out British tribes from the north. Sometimes these tribes caused trouble in the Roman part of Britain.

Parts of Hadrian's Wall can still be seen today.

Source B

The remains of Hadrian's Wall

The Romans Leave Britain

The Romans ruled Britain for about four hundred years. But then Rome itself came under attack. In the year 410 the Romans and their army left Britain. The soldiers went back to defend their homes in Rome.

Many Britons tried to carry on living like they had when the Romans were in charge. But soon other invaders were conquering parts of Britain.

'Hold Out' on Hadrians Wall

Play this game and find out what it was like to be a soldier on Hadrian's Wall.

You will need:

- 2–4 players
- dice or numbered papers (1–6)

Each player is a 'centurion' – a Roman soldier in charge of 100 men.

Aim

You and your men have to defend one mile of Hadrian's Wall in the dark for five nights. (Monday–Friday)

You have to stop raiders getting across the wall. This would be easy in the summer. But now it is the middle of winter. Some nights are freezing cold. The wind and snow blow across the dark wall.

Many soldiers will catch 'frostbite' if you use them all to patrol. So you have to risk as few soldiers as possible but still defend the wall. Each centurion has a different part of the wall to defend. You will win points if you manage to keep the raiders out. But you will lose points if a lot of your men get frostbite. The centurion who does best will get promotion and six months holiday back in sunny Rome.

The one who does worst will have to spend the rest of the winter 'on the wall'.

Before You Play

Make a copy of the 'Regiment Report' below. Use
this to keep a record of your progress.

Regiment Report

	Example	Monday	Tuesday	Wednesday	Thursday	Friday
Number of men on duty	60					
Weather (f = freezing / w = warm)	f					
Are there any frosty soldiers? (yes/no)	yes					
Number of points lost for frosty soldiers (see table A)	− 6	—	—	—	—	—
Number of tribes attacking (1–6)	3					
Number of soldiers needed to defend your section (see table B)	40					
Did you hold out? (yes/no)	yes					
Win 20 points if you held out	+ 20	+	+	+	+	+
Total points	+ 14					

How to Play

Monday Night

STEP 1

Each centurion decide how many men you are going to use on patrol tonight: 20, 30, 40, 60, 80, or 100.

(Remember! If you use a lot of men it will be easy to defend the wall BUT you risk more men getting frostbite if it is a cold night.)

Make your decisions. Fill in line 1 of your 'Regiment Report' for Monday.

STEP 2

When all the centurions are ready throw the dice. (once only!) This will tell you the weather tonight for all parts of the wall.

1/2/3 = Warm weather, no problem.
4/5/6 = Freezing weather.

If the weather is freezing some of your men will get frostbite so you lose points. Look at Table A. This will tell you how many points you have lost.

Fill in the next 3 lines of your Report.

STEP 3

When everyone is ready throw the dice again. This time every centurion throws in turn. This will tell you the strength of tonight's attack by raiding tribesmen. (6 = strong attack, 1 = weak attack)

Look at Table B. This will tell you how many soldiers you will need to fight them off. Have you got enough soldiers on patrol? Did you hold out? If so gain 20 points. If not gain no points.

Fill the the rest of the lines in your Report. (Look at your scores between the thick lines to work out your total points for Monday night.)

Repeat these steps for Tuesday, Wednesday, Thursday and Friday nights.

The winner is the centurion with the most points at the end.

Table A: Points lost on a cold night

Number of men on duty	Points lost
20	2
40	4
60	6
80	8
100	10

Table B: Points won for defending the wall

Strength of attack	1	2	3	4	5	6
Number of soldiers needed to defend your section	10	20	40	60	80	100

If you keep the raiders out gain 20 points.
If they break through, gain 0 points.

WORKFILE

1 Write two or three sentences to answer these questions about the game.

a Who was the best centurion in your group? Why do you think they won?
b Who was the worst centurion in your group? Why do you think they lost?
c Do you think the Roman soldiers enjoyed their duty on the wall? Explain your answer.

2 Draw a picture of yourself defending the wall.

New Invaders

It is the year 800 AD. Britain has changed a lot in the 400 years since the Romans left.

1 Most Roman buildings have fallen into ruin. No one knows how to repair them.

2 Angle and Saxon people from Europe invaded most of southern Britain after the Romans left.

repair, **Angle, Saxon, kingdom, Viking,** progress, timeline

3 Parts of Britain have been divided into several Anglo/Saxon kingdoms.

New invaders now threaten these kingdoms. They are the **Vikings** from the north of Europe.

WORKFILE

1 Copy the boxes below. See if you can unscramble the letters to make correct words. The first letter of each word has been underlined to help you.

a Four groups of people who invaded Britain:

mn<u>r</u>aos	gk<u>v</u>iisn	xn<u>s</u>oas	<u>n</u>lsage

b Three Anglo/Saxon kingdoms (look back at the drawing):

<u>m</u>rieca	sse<u>w</u>x	s<u>s</u>eusx

2 Throughout history things have often got better. There have been new inventions and ideas. This is called progress.

The table below shows you how some progress has been made in recent times.

Copy the table and complete the second column by choosing your answers from those below:

- 'We can travel quickly by jet aeroplane.'
- 'Doctors can use laser beams.'
- 'We can listen to CD players.'
- 'They can use a calculator.'

3 But sometimes in the past there has been no progress. Sometimes things have even got worse.

Look at page 25. Write a sentence or two to explain one time in the past when things got worse. (Clue . . . Roman building skills.)

4 How are things getting worse nowadays? Crime? Pollution? See if you (and your group) can make a list of at least 10 things.

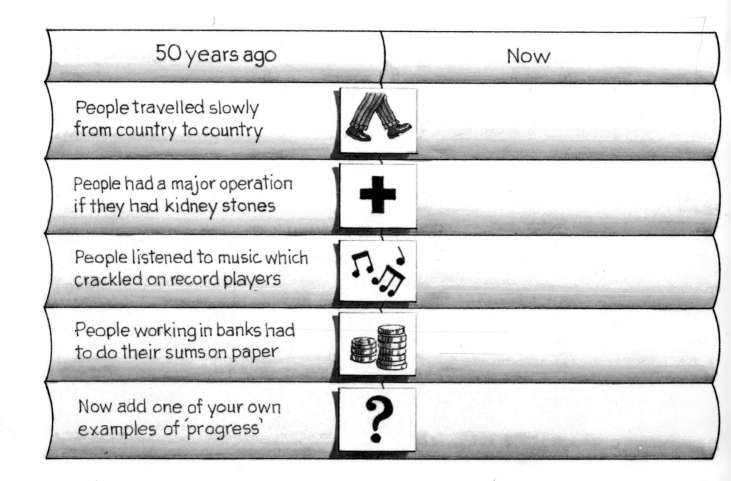

50 years ago	Now
People travelled slowly from country to country	
People had a major operation if they had kidney stones	
People listened to music which crackled on record players	
People working in banks had to do their sums on paper	
Now add one of your own examples of 'progress'	

5 The table on the right shows who ruled Britain and when between the years 43 and 800. But the time periods are not in the right order. Each period of time should follow on from the last one. Try to sort them out. Copy the table in the correct order.

Colour each time period in your table with a different colour.

Time Period	What Happened
400–550	Anglo Saxons slowly take over country after much fighting
43–400	Romans ruled Britain
550–800	Anglo-Saxon kings ruled Britain

Timeline

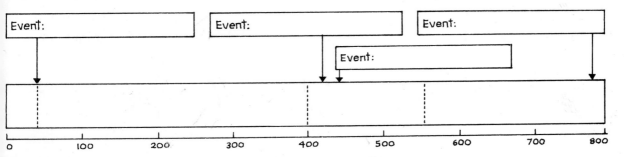

WORKFILE

6 The timeline above shows you some more events but it needs to be labelled.

    a Copy the timeline. Take care to space out the years properly. Leave room for the event boxes but do not copy them yet.

b Notice that the timeline has been divided up into time periods. These are the same time periods you used in your table. (See question 5.) Colour in the periods on your timeline using the same colours you used before.

c Now add the event boxes to your timeline. Choose from the events on the right. Use the year to help you decide which box to put each event in.

Event year : 43

Romans invade Britain.

Event year : 410

Romans army leaves Britain.

Event year : 428

First Anglo Saxons come to live in Britain.

Event year : 790

Vikings raid Anglo Saxon kingdoms.

10

A History Mystery

Trying to find out what Anglo Saxon Britain was like is not easy. There are not many clues. Not much evidence.

Archaeologists have found old Anglo Saxon settlements in the countryside but no buildings remain. Only holes in the ground.

Sometimes they have also found ashes and animal bones.

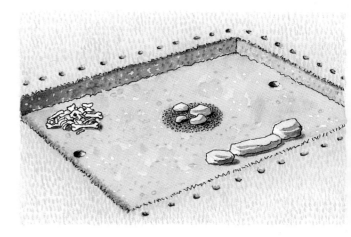

Source A

The remains of an Anglo Saxon house found at Sutton Hoo

Archaeologists have also found Anglo Saxon graves. One site at Sutton Hoo is very famous. There they found a Saxon king buried in his ship. They found many other things too that were buried with him.

Source B

Archaeologists at work on the Sutton Hoo ship

A gold buckle found at Sutton Hoo

WORKFILE

1 Look at the table below. In the left hand column are some statements about Anglo Saxon evidence.

In the right hand column are some statements about what the evidence proves. But these are jumbled up. Copy the table and see if you can match up each pair of statements.

Evidence	This might show that . . .
A helmet was found at Sutton Hoo	Anglo Saxon metal workers were very skilled
A gold buckle was found at Sutton Hoo	Anglo Saxons built houses of wood, not stone
No remains of houses were found on the sites of Anglo Saxon settlements	Anglo Saxon warriors wore armour

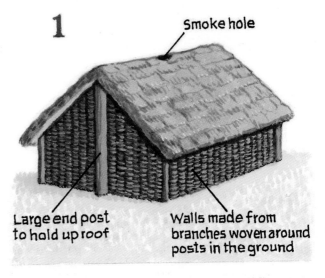

1 Smoke hole

Large end post to hold up roof

Walls made from branches woven around posts in the ground

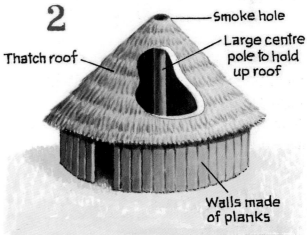

2 Smoke hole

Large centre pole to hold up roof

Thatch roof

Walls made of planks

2 Look carefully at Source A. We do not know exactly what an Anglo Saxon hut looked like but we can guess. Can you work it out?

Choose one of the huts opposite. Pick the one which you think best fits the evidence in Source A.

(Do the others in your group agree with you?)

Remember!

– No building materials were found. Whatever they used had rotted away long ago.

– Settlements were often built in forests.

a Draw the hut you think best fits the evidence in Source A. Do not forget the labels.

b Write two or three sentences to say why you did not choose the other two types of houses.

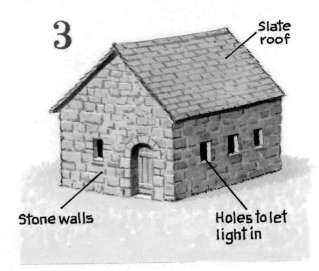

3 Slate roof

Stone walls

Holes to let light in

Source C

History Jury

A helmet, decorated with bronze, silver and bright stones, found at Sutton Hoo

Look at the evidence in sources A, B, C and D. Decide what they prove.

You are acting like the jury in a court room. Think about each of the statements below. Which ones should we believe? How does the evidence prove them to be true or false?

(Do the others in your group agree with you?)

- Anglo Saxons built fine stone palaces like the Romans. .
- Anglo Saxons lived in wooden huts.
- Anglo Saxons were good sailors.
- Anglo Saxons did not know much about working with metals.
- Anglo Saxons were vegetarians.
- Anglo Saxons lived in large towns.

a Make two lists of the statements above. In one list put those you think are true. In the other put those you think are false.

b Choose two of these statements. Write a sentence or two about each one. Say why you think it is true or false. What evidence have you used to prove your case?

Source D

A decorated purse-lid, also from Sutton Hoo

The Angles and Saxons Arrive

North Sea, **longship, raided**

1/The Angles and Saxons crossed the North Sea to Britain in longships. Small groups of ships sailed up British rivers. They raided British towns and took away treasure and slaves.

2/Later more came. They wanted land to live on.

3/The Britons fought back but slowly the Anglo Saxons took over much of the south of Britain. They set up their own kingdoms.

WORKFILE

1 Copy these sentences and fill in the missing words. Choose from the words at the beginning of each section.

a invasion, took, Small, farming, Some.

The Anglo Saxon invasion was not like the Roman _____ of Britain. They did not bring one large army. _____ groups of ships raided the coasts and rivers.

They _____ away slaves and treasure from the old Roman towns. _____ Anglo Saxons stayed in Britain. They had found good _____ land. Other groups came to join them.

b many, kingdoms, and, Britons.

The _____ tried to stop them but they were beaten in _____ small battles.

Angles _____ Saxons took over southern Britain. They set up their own _____ .

2 Write two or three sentences to say in your own words why the Anglo Saxons wanted to live in Britain.

Naming the New Land

language, place name, natural features, **stockade**

A New Language

The Angles and Saxons spoke their own language. When they found a new place to settle they gave it a new name.

Many of our place names come from old Anglo Saxon words–Birmingham and Southampton, for example.

The part of Britain they took over also took on a new name. It was called Angle Lang (England).

Their language developed into the one we all speak, English.

Place Names

Many places were named after natural features. Some names were Anglo Saxon words for town or settlement. Look at Source A. It shows what we think some Anglo Saxon words might have meant. See if you can work out what they were. Use the list of 'meanings' below to help you.

(Do the others in your group agree with you?)

Possible Meanings

- 'A small settlement or homestead (one or two families).'
- 'A crossing through a river or stream.
- 'A larger settlement. Often surrounded by a wooden stockade or fence.'
- 'A clearing in the forest.'

Source A

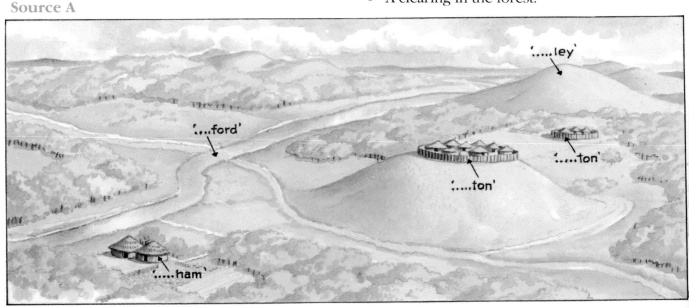

WORKFILE

1 Copy and complete the table below. Use it to show what you have decided each Anglo Saxon word means.

Anglo Saxon word	Meaning
_____ ley	
_____ ton	
_____ ford	
_____ ham	

2 Look at Source B. This is a map of the same area of the country. The place names are now given in full. Use the Anglo Saxon dictionary below to work out what each full name might have meant.

Use the words you have just used in question 1 as well. (Do the others in your group agree with you?)

Example: Trentham = Trent, the name of a
river + ham, a
homestead.

So Trentham means a homestead by the river Trent.

Anglo Saxon Dictionary

Han   = high land.
Han   = a persons name.
Trent = the name of a river.
Blur   = open and windy hill.
Fen   = wet and marshy low ground.

Notice that the word Han has two meanings. You should choose the one that best fits what you can see in Source A.

Source B

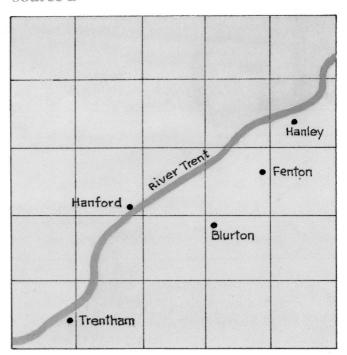

3 Copy and complete a placename box for each of the places on the map.
- Write in the placename.
- Write in A1, A2 and so on to show which square on the map the place appears in.
- Write in the modern English meaning of the placename. For example:

Placename	Trentham
Map square	A1
This name means	a homestead by the river Trent

4 Make a list of as many places you can think of which have Anglo Saxon endings like ham, ton, ford, or ley.

They may be near your home or far away. Here are three to start you off: Birmingham, Southampton, Burnley.

13

A Time of Change

gods, **pagan**, beliefs, **Christian, goddess**

As time goes by some things change a lot and some things change very little. In Anglo Saxon England a very important change took place. This change still affects our life now, over one thousand years later.

A Change of Belief

Gods were very important to the Anglo Saxons. Before the change we are looking at they were pagans. They believed in many different gods. These gods ruled the natural world, the sky, forests and moon.

It took a long time for change to happen. But many Anglo Saxons changed their beliefs. They became 'Christians'. Now they believed in only one all powerful God.

WORKFILE

1 Think about things which change as time passes. Copy the table below. Decide how things have changed since Anglo Saxon times. Put a tick in the column you think is correct.

Has it changed?	Changed a lot	Not changed much
Travel from place to place		
Mountains		
Rivers		
Houses		
Music		
Clothes		
Beliefs		

2 Study the picture on the left. It was found on an old Anglo Saxon helmet. Which god might it be? Choose from the following pagan gods.

- 'Eostre', the moon goddess.
- 'Thor', the god of thunder, lightning and the sky.
- 'Woden', the magical king of all the gods.
- 'Tiw', the god of war.

Draw the picture and put a title.

Spreading the New Beliefs

caused, persuade, **baptised, mission**

We now know that a great change took place in Anglo Saxon England. Why did this happen? Here is the story of what caused many people to change from their old beliefs.

Year 597 in the Kingdom of Kent. England is still a pagan country. Bertha brings a message to her husband King Ethelbert

Augustine has arrived with a group of monks. He brings greetings from Pope Gregory in Rome.

I don't trust these Christians. Their magic is too powerful.

Tell him I will meet him, but only outside in the open air.

Queen Bertha was not a pagan. She came from Gaul, a Christian Kingdom

Will you let his monks speak to the people? They could use my own small church.

Well, I'm not sure that's a good idea

Please!

Er, I suppose so

The monks tour Kent while Augustine tries to persuade Ethelbert to change his beliefs

Ethelbert is baptised as a Christian. Many people in Kent follow his example

And in East Anglia....

Is our King Raedwald going to take up this new belief or not?

Yes, but he's keeping the temples to the old gods too – just in case

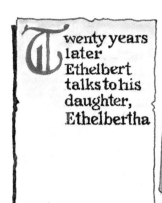

WORKFILE

1 Look at the table. It shows some important facts taken from the picture strip. See if you can find which box number each one is taken from.

The first one is done for you. Copy and complete the table.

Event	Box Number
The Pope wanted to change England to a Christian country.	1
Some kings did not like to drop the old gods.	
Some kingdoms stayed pagan.	
Two kings were baptised as Christians.	
King Ethelbert had heard about Christians before Augustine landed.	

2 This picture shows Augustine arriving in Kent at the start of the story. Study the flow chart opposite. It shows some of the events you have read about. But they are not in the correct order. Sort them out. Put them in the order they happened. Copy the flow chart in the right order. Number the boxes 1–6.

Ethelbertha and Paulinius take the new beliefs to Northumbria.

King Edwin and Coifi are baptised at York.

Augustine arrives in Kent on a mission from Rome.

King Ethelbert is baptised at Canterbury.

Edwin is killed in battle.

3 What caused people to change belief? Sometimes changes have causes. There are reasons why a change takes place. See if you can work out some causes. Why did some people in England change belief? Copy each of the sentences below. Write 'true' or 'false' at the end of each one to show what you think. (Do the others in your group agree with you?)

Change took place because:

a Christians came to England to spread their message.
b People were paid a lot of money to change.
c People thought that the new beliefs were better.
d People were unhappy with the old gods.
e Important women persuaded kings to change.
f Christians beat the pagans in battle.

14 *Christian Northumbria*

monk, saint, miracle, monastery, effects

Northumbria stayed Christian after Edwin died. Many monks came from Scotland to Northumbria. They were led by a monk called Aiden. They lived simple lives. They taught ordinary people about God. Some of these monks became famous. Like Aiden they were made saints after their death.

One was named Saint Cuthbert. He was said to have cured people using miracles. One story said that when his feet were wet wild animals came to him. They dried his feet with their fur.

The monks built monasteries to live in and churches to pray in. They learned to build using stone like the Romans had done.

This stone church still stands in the north of England. It was built about 1100 years ago.

Escomb Church, Durham

Otters dry Saint Cuthbert's feet with their fur

Monks lived a hard life. They wore simple clothes. They spent their time praying and writing books about their belief.

Northumbria became very well known for its books. One book in particular is very famous, *The History of The English Church and People* by a monk called Bede. Much of what we know about Anglo Saxon England comes from this book.

So, a lot of things happened after Northumbria became a Christian kingdom.

WORKFILE

1 Copy and complete these sentences by filling in the names of famous monks you have read about here.

a _____ was said to have performed miracles.

b _____ wrote the first English history book.

c _____ brought Christianity to Northumbria from Scotland.

2 When a change takes place new things happen as a result. These are called effects. The first diagram below shows a change which you will have lived through. It also shows some of the new things which might have happened to you – the effects on you.

a Copy the diagram adding two more effects of your own.

b Think of another change which has affected you, such as changing house or changing car. See if you can think of three effects of that change. Draw a diagram like the first one.

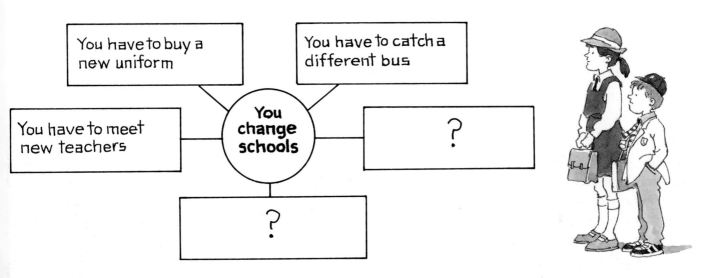

3 We know many people in Northumbria became Christians. What were the effects on life in Northumbria? Draw a diagram like the one below. But only copy those effects you think *really* happened. (Do the others in your group agree with your choice?)

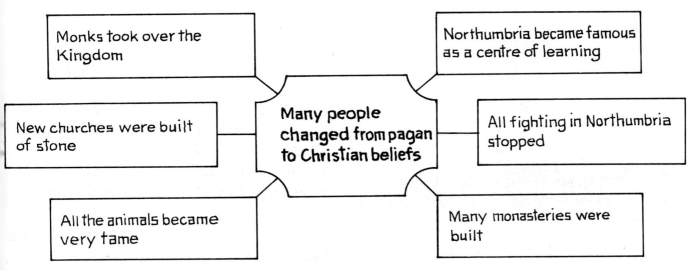

15 *People From the North*

He was good at fighting using an axe or sword. His people thought it was very important for a boy to be a skilled and brave warrior. Sometimes families fell out with each other and fought to see who was best.

The people from this part of the world had many names. They are usually known as Vikings.

Viking weapons

Helmet

Axeheads

Swords and spearhead

Meet Sven. He was 17 years old in the year 800. He had two sisters and two older brothers.

He did not live in Britain. He lived in Scandinavia. You can see his home village marked on the map. His was a land of forests and cold seas. There was some good farm land there but not very much.

Sven learnt how to grow crops, and how to make things out of wood. Sven's country had a long coastline. Many of his people got their food from the sea by fishing. They were expert sailors and built some of the best ships in the world. These ships were fast, strong and very seaworthy.

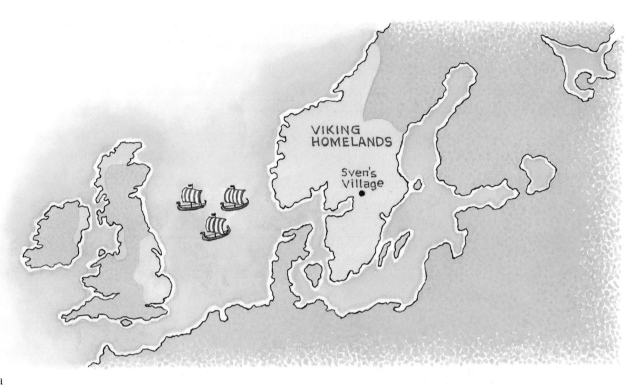

Scandinavia

WORKFILE

1 Match the beginnings of the following words with their endings. They tell you some of the names which we use now for the lands where the Vikings came from.

Nor den
Swe mark
Den way

2 Draw a labelled picture of Sven, called 'Sven the Viking'. Use these labels:

tunic made from wool, leather cross garters, staff.

3 Think about the things which Viking boys were taught.

 a Make a list of five things which Vikings thought were important to teach their children, such as *fishing*.

 b Make a list of five things which you have been taught, such as *reading and writing*.

 c Most of the skills you have been taught are different to those taught to Viking boys. Can you think why? (Do the others in your group agree with you?)
Write a sentence or two to explain.

 d Which Viking skill would you most like to learn? Draw a picture of yourself doing it. Write a speech bubble to explain why you are enjoying it.

 e Viking boys were expected to be brave. What do you think is the most important thing for you to be? Choose one from the following: brave, clever, honest, hardworking, reliable, friendly.

 (Do the others in your group agree with you?)

 Write a sentence or two to explain what you think and why.

4 Look at the Viking weapons on page 40. Draw each of the weapons and put a title with each one. Use these titles:

axe, helmet, spear head, sword.

Viking Poems

The quotes below are taken from an old Viking poem. It gave advice to young Vikings about how to live. We can learn a lot from this about the way Vikings thought. Read each quote. Then read the box underneath. Choose which answer in the box best suits the line from the poem. (Do the others in you group agree with you?)

quote, reputation

WORKFILE

Copy each of the quotes below and underneath write the correct answer from the box.

---

a 'When a guest arrives cold after crossing the mountain he needs fire, food and clothing.'

a) Vikings were very unfriendly
b) Vikings looked after their friends.

b 'A man ought never to leave his weapons even when in the fields.'

a) Vikings might be attacked at any time.
b) Vikings looked for fights all the time.

c 'A man who plans on taking his neighbour's life and property should get up early.'

a) Only Viking thieves get up early.
b) Vikings thought it was OK to kill and steal sometimes.

d 'We shall all die one day but one thing will never die. The reputation a man leaves behind.'

Vikings should
a) try to make a good name for themselves.
b) tell everyone how good they are.

16

Viking Longships

design, developed, **trade, fleet**

The Vikings had learned to build ships which were far better than other ships at that time. Larger, stronger and much faster. The design of the wooden ships developed over a long time. The picture below shows a typical Viking longship which was buried in Norway in the tenth century.

Vikings sailed to many parts of Europe in these ships. It is likely they even sailed to North America. Sometimes they sailed to other lands to trade. To buy and sell goods. Sometimes they sailed to raid, to steal treasure. Sometimes they sailed in large fleets to conquer parts of other lands. They were always proud of the fine ships which carried them swiftly across the waves.

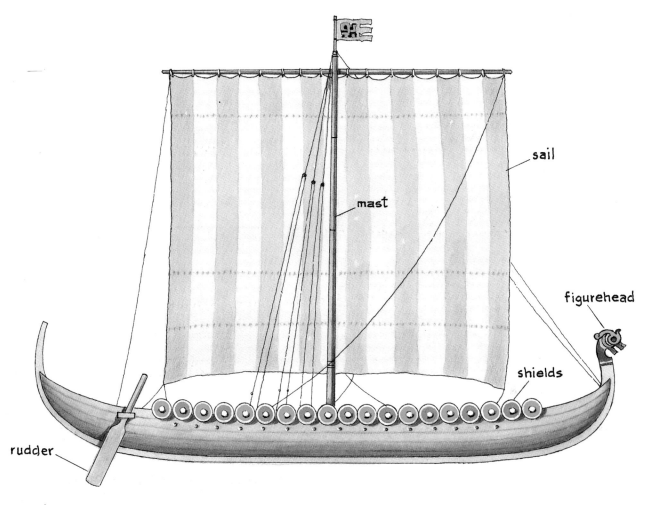

A Viking longship

This drawing shows you some of the important parts of the ship.

WORKFILE

1 Look at the drawing of a Viking longship. Make your own drawing of a longship. Label your drawing like the one above.

2 Look at this table. The right column shows some of the parts of a ship. The left column describes what each part was used for. But they do not match. See if you can match the correct part with the description in the left column. Copy the table correctly.

Description	Part of ship
Used to steer ship	sail
Tied to side of boat for protection. Could be taken off and carried ashore when fighting	figurehead
Wooden pole about ten metres tall used to hold up sail	rudder
Carving at front of boat used to frighten enemies	shields
Made from strips of woollen cloth	mast

replica

Daily Lies   September 1999

VIKING VOYAGE.

WANTED!

Young people to sail to America in a replica of a Viking ship. It should take about three weeks. No modern items on board. You will have to live and dress like the Vikings did. Good wages paid. Your chance to appear on T.V.

Suppose this advert appeared in your local paper. How would you feel about going on this voyage? Look carefully at the pictures on this page and the next before answering the questions in the boxes.

(Talk over each of them with the others in your group.)

Sea conditions . . .

- What would happen in a storm or in large waves?
- What would happen if it was very hot?

Food . . .

- What would you eat?
- How would it be kept fresh?
- How would it be cooked?
- What would you drink?

Navigation . . .

- How would you know where to go?
- What would happen if it was foggy?

Washing . . .

- Where would you wash yourselves and your clothes?
- Where are the toilets?

Comfort . . .

- Where would you sit and sleep?

WORKFILE

1 a Write down three reasons why the voyage might be dangerous.

b Write down three reasons why the voyage might be uncomfortable.

c Write down three reasons why you might want to go.

d Write down three jobs you might be asked to do on board ship.

2 Do you think the Vikings felt the same way as you would about their voyages?

Copy this table. Put a tick beside each statement to say whether you think it is true or false.

Statement	True	False
Vikings were tough so they would not mind being uncomfortable as much as me.		
Vikings were brave so they would be less scared than me.		
Vikings had a different reason than mine for suffering the hard voyage.		
Vikings were used to adventure so they would not get as excited as me when they set off.		

3 Do you think all Vikings felt the same about their voyages? Write a sentence or two to show how each of the following Vikings might feel as their ship left their homeland.

a A young Viking on his first voyage.

b An older Viking who has made many voyages before.

18 The Vikings in England

Danegeld, Danelaw

Vikings first raided England around the year 800. Monasteries were their favourite target. There was lots of gold to take. The monks were men of peace who did not fight back. Many monks were killed.

Then bigger groups of Vikings raided towns. More and more Vikings came as time went by. Viking armies defeated Anglo Saxon kings in many battles.

Some kings paid large sums of money called 'Danegeld' to the Vikings. They hoped the Vikings would go away and leave them in peace. The Vikings left but soon came back for more 'Danegeld'.

King Alfred of Wessex fought back against the Vikings. He was known as Alfred the Great. His army beat the Vikings in battle in the year 878.

The Danelaw

England was then divided into two parts. Wessex was ruled by Alfred the Great. The Vikings ruled the part they called the 'Danelaw'. The two sides stopped fighting for many years.

Then the English King Ethelred tried to get rid of the Vikings from the Danelaw. The Vikings fought back and won. Now they ruled all of the country. The Viking Cnut became king in 1016. He was the first king to rule over all of England.

History Jury

Sometimes we can learn a lot about people by looking at their actions. What can we learn about Vikings from what you have just read? What do their actions prove?

Look at these five boxes. Copy three which you think are true. With each one write a sentence or two. Say what the Vikings did which proves it was true. (Do the others in your group agree with you?)

Vikings were not Christians.

Vikings did not like living in England.

Vikings were poor fighters.

There was not enough land for everyone in the Viking homelands.

Vikings thought England was a good island to raid.

A statue of
Alfred the Great

WORKFILE

1 Unscramble these words. The first letter of each word has been underlined. Copy them with their clues.

clue	word
a Taken from monasteries	lgod
b Many killed by Vikings	nks<u>m</u>o
c A great king	rlf<u>A</u>ed
d Paid to Vikings to stop them fighting	lnaeg<u>D</u>ed
e Viking part of England	<u>D</u>nlaeaw

2 Draw a map of England and show the Danelaw.

3 Copy and complete these sentences. Choose the correct endings from those in brackets.
   a Vikings first raided England around the year _____ (200, 800, 1000).
   b Alfred's army beat the Vikings in _____ (187, 678, 878).
   c Cnut became King of all England in _____ (1016, 1066, 1106).

4 Draw your own timeline. Show the correct three dates above. Say what happened. Look at the timeline you did on page 27 to help you.